Bygone
BILLINGSGATE

Fish filleting competition.

Bygone
BILLINGSGATE

Colin Manton
and
John Edwards

Phillimore

1989

Published by
PHILLIMORE & CO. LTD.
Shopwyke Hall, Chichester, Sussex

ISBN 0 85033 689 9

Printed and bound in Great Britain by
BIDDLES LTD.
Guildford, Surrey

List of Illustrations

Frontispiece: Fish filleting competition

Photographs

All photographs are copyright of the Museum of London.

Acknowledgements

The authors are very grateful to the Museum of London for permission to undertake this book and to reproduce the photographs and thank Valerie Cumming, Deputy Director of the Museum, for her help and advice.

The authors thank David Butcher, Billingsgate Superintendent, for permission to photograph in the market and for his helpful tour of the premises and informative comments.

Thanks are also due to the many firms and indviduals at Billingsgate Market who provided special access for photography, or gave interviews, including the Fishmongers' Company; the London Fish Merchants' Association; Smithers and Skinner Ltd.; Brice Bros.; P.F. Farmer Ltd.; John Koch Ltd.; Billingsgate Overall Services; J. Williams and Son.; Pauline Brillus; Sister Davey and Messrs Watkin, Francis, Old, Flood, Stearman, Tyler, Foulger, Seagrave, Farmer, Gibbard, Shiells and Branch.

The comments of Christopher Ellmers and Patricia O'Driscoll on aspects of Billingsgate's history are much appreciated. Finally, the assistance of the staff of the Guildhall Library is acknowledged with thanks.

Introduction

Popularly accepted as offering the best choice of fresh fish in the world, Billingsgate was also regarded as London's most picturesque and historic market. As much a landmark as nearby London Bridge, Billingsgate was a very special place. The public associated it with the pervasive odour of fish and the colourful language of the porters. In the trade, Billingsgate was renowned for speed and dependability combined with the unrivalled freshness and variety of its wares.

Once Billingsgate seemed as unchanging as the River Thames which ebbed and flowed against the wooden piles of its old wharf. All around the market, however, London was changing at an accelerating rate. As the 20th century progressed, more traffic was generated on already inadequate roads. Billingsgate struggled with the problems of its restricted site for over a century. Market vehicles had nowhere to park, except in the surrounding streets, which became hopelessly congested. A planning decision to upgrade Lower Thames Street into a fast dual carriageway, running across the market's doorstep, finally made trade impossible at Billingsgate. In 1982 the market left its ancient site for new premises on the Isle of Dogs, in London's Docklands.

Billingsgate's imposing Victorian market building survived but conversion for banking use inevitably changed its old character. The distinctive atmosphere which the fish trade once contributed to Billingsgate completely disappeared. With the market's removal, over one thousand years of trading was brought to an end.

History

Although long associated with the fish trade, Billingsgate began life in the distant past as a small port handling general cargo. It first evolved as one of a series of 'hithes' or inlets in the northern bank of the Thames which protected small vessels as they unloaded. As the name implies, the hithe was one of the old 'watergates' of the city. The name is also evidence of its Saxon foundation. According to Stow, Billingsgate, like neighbouring wharves, was named after its owner, in this case, a Saxon called Biling or Beling.[1] Strype quoted payment of landing tolls at Billingsgate in the late Saxon era, confirming the port's early prominence.[2] Archaeological evidence recently uncovered indicates that Billingsgate was probably established even earlier than commonly accepted, in Roman times.[3] Geoffrey of Monmouth's fanciful tale of a much older foundation by a mythical king of the Britons, Belin, although intriguing to antiquarians, can be safely dismissed.[4] It took many centuries, however, for Billingsgate to become synonymous with fish. The neighbouring port of Queenhithe, upstream of old London Bridge, was once far more favoured and, as the name implies, enjoyed royal patronage. For example, in 1227 King Henry III ordered all fish landed elsewhere to be seized. Even in the 15th century Queenhithe took the lion's share of fish catches. Landings were only permitted at Billingsgate if more than one fishing vessel was waiting to unload. Cargoes of coal, corn, wine and other provisions were generally sent to Billingsgate.[5]

Nevertheless, Queenhithe's early monopoly of fish deliveries ultimately had important consequences for Billingsgate's prosperity, largely because of its close proximity. The fish markets, which naturally grew up in the streets around Queenhithe where the fish arrived, expanded eastwards, stretching along Thames Street and reaching Billingsgate itself by the end of the 14th century.[6] Billingsgate was therefore in an ideal position to exploit the fish trade when the port of Queenhithe fell on bad times.

The reasons for Queenhithe's decline were various but, apart from royal patronage, it had few practical advantages. it was badly situated and was obstructed by Old London Bridge. This not only presented a serious hazard to smaller boats navigating the treacherous currents between the piers but also formed an impassable barrier when cargo vessels became larger. Eventually ships were obliged to anchor downstream of the bridge, transferring cargoes to smaller lighters which landed at appropriate specialised wharves along the north bank, including Billingsgate.

Fish landings became concentrated at Billingsgate for several reasons. Firstly, since fish was highly perishable and had to be sold quickly, it made sense to send it to Billingsgate which already adjoined a fish market. Secondly, many fishing boats were small enough conveniently to enter the hithe direct and unload. Thirdly, because fish was easily damaged and needed special handling, it would have been a mistake to have mixed catches with general cargoes at other landing places.

By the beginning of the 17th century, Queenhithe was 'almost forsaken'[7] whilst Billingsgate had become London's 'larder door' even for fish. Stow noted '... shippes and boats commonly arriuing there with fish both fresh and salt, shellfishes. salt, Orenges, Onions and other fruits and rootes, wheate, Rie and graine of diuers sorts for seruice of the Citie, and the parts of this Realme adioyning'.[8]

In parallel with these events, the Corporation of London, in partnership with the powerful Fishmongers' Company, sought to bring wholesale fish markets under better regulation. The Fishmongers' Company, one of the 12 great Livery Companies of the City, received its first charter from Edward I in 1272. In the 14th century the Company secured a monopoly on the sale of fish, a valuable privilege since this was one of the most important necessities of medieval Londoners' diet. Both the City and the Company recognised the importance of ensuring fair prices for consumers, preventing abuses of trade and checking that corrupt fish was not sold at irregular markets, which would have been difficult to inspect. Centralisation of the wholoesale fish trade at Billingsgate provided the solution to improved supervision. It was not the complete answer as, apparently, certain unscrupulous fishmongers persisted in sharp practices. These included 'forestalling', that is, buying up fish supplies to their advantage before catches had even reached the market, and 'engrossing', in other words, employing members to buy up all the fish at the market itself, distributing this amongst themselves in lots and selling at exorbitant prices.

Eventually recognising that more determined measures were necessary, the Corporation secured an Act of Parliament unequivocally establishing a 'free and open' fish market at Billingsgate. This momentous Act of 1698 created an indissoluble union between the fish trade and Billingsgate and outlawed trading cliques. '... Billingsgate having time out of mind been a Free Market for all manner of Floating and Salt fish ... (it was enacted) ... that after the Tenth Day of May 1699 Billingsgate Market within the said City of London shall be every Day in the week [except Sundays] a free and open Market for all sorts of Fish whatsoever ...'[9]

Although it was indelibly associated with fish from that date, further enactments proved necessary to bring Billingsgate effectively under City governance and to provide for the construction of a market hall to deal with the massively increased volume of trade as London's population expanded. The exploitation of new fishing grounds and the adoption of modern methods of fish deliveries were also to have a profound effect on market organisation.

The Billingsgate familiar to recent generations of market workers, customers, visitors and observers of London was a very different world in 1698. The old dock survived until the 1840s and fishing boats continued to unload their catches. Surprisingly, though, for a market which was the focus of London's huge fish trade, there was no trading hall until the 1850s. Fish selling was conducted in primitive wooden sheds.

1. An aquatint of Billingsgate market, 1808, by Pugin and Rowlandson. This illustrates the appearance of Billingsgate Dock from Thames Street, including the stout figures of the market's redoubtable fishwives.

It must be confessed that the area once had an unsavoury reputation and never quite lost its association with bad language. Boisterous drinkers and shady characters frequented the rough taverns of nearby Dark House Lane, especially the notorious Darkhouse itself, later swept away by Victorian improvements. Regulars included seamen, watermen, labourers, petty criminals, rakes and, of course, the sharp-tongued Billingsgate fishwives, '... fat motherly flat-caps with their fish-baskets hanging upon their heads instead of riding hoods, with every one her nipperkin of warm ale and brandy and as many rings upon their thumbs as belongs to a set of bed curtains; everyone as slender in the waist as a Dutch skipper in the buttocks and together, looking like a litter of squab elephants. Their noses were as sharp as the gnomon of a dial and looked as blue as if they had been frost-nipped.'[10] Ned Ward described how he and a friend thought better of their foray to the Darkhouse after a night on the town. Both fled the vicious insults of the fishwives, surmising that '... if their talons were as sharp as their tongues, they need not fear a combat with all the beasts of America'![11]

A much later generation of respectable Victorian observers such as Henry Mayhew took comfort in assurances that there was far less blasphemy. Language was racy but usually good humoured. Understandably, common politenesses were sometimes difficult to observe when manhandling heavy fish boxes through the crowded market.

Billingsgate in the 1840s retained a distinctly nautical air. 'The passenger, as he crosses London Bridge, if he looks eastward, on the northern bank of the river will notice a little copse of masts at the west end of the Custom House. They indicate the situation of Billingsgate, the only wholesale market in the metropolis for the sale of fish.'[12]

George Augustus Sala was far from complimentary about the situation itself, describing an '... unclean old batch of sheds and hovels, reeking with fishy smells ... '[13] To Mayhew, Billingsgate was crowded, dark and dirty but colourful and fascinating. 'The wooden barn-looking square where the fish is sold, is soon after six o'clock crowded with shiny cord jackets and greasy caps. Everyone comes to Billingsgate in his worst clothes and no-one knows the length of time a coat can be worn until they have been to a fish sale. Through the bright opening at the end are seen the tangled rigging of the oyster-boats and the red worsted caps of the sailors.'[14]

2. J.B. Bunning's watercolour of Billingsgate market, 1851. It shows the 'Italian' facade fronting the Thames and porters unloading fishing vessels.

Acts passed in 1846 and 1871 subsequently brought the market under complete control of the 'Mayor and Commonalty and Citizens of the City of London'. In practice, this meant Billingsgate was run by the Markets Committee of the Corporation which appointed a Billingsgate Superintendent for day to day management. Rents were charged for market accommodation and tolls collected on fish cargoes landed. A special force of market police enforced the market byelaws, directed local traffic and prevented pilfering.

Billingsgate Dock was filled in to create more space for the growing market and a new, purpose-built trading hall was completed in 1850 by the City Architect, J.B.Bunning.[15] These so-called 'commodious buildings with the pleasing Italian facade'[16] improved the river frontage where fish was landed but did little for the market's landward appearance. Few of the facilities required by a modern market were incorporated and the building proved too small for the rapid expansion of business. A much enlarged market hall designed by a notable later City Architect, Sir Horace Jones, replaced the earlier building in 1877. This continued in use until Billingsgate's final closure over a century later. Construction was a massive and expensive undertaking which, in many respects, overcame the disadvantages of the site and offered improved accommodation and new facilities. Limitations imposed by Custom House to the east and valuable wharves to the west were compensated for by absorbing old Dark House Lane and Billingsgate Stairs, yielding a further enlarged area between Thames Street and the river. With admirable thoroughness, Sir Horace ensured the future stability of the building by excavating the shifting subsoil to depths varying from 15 feet to 50 feet beneath Thames Street to guarantee firm foundations. Walls adjoining the site were underpinned 50 feet to prevent the possibility of subsidence.

The new market hall offered advanced features for the era, including steam-powered lifts. The steam generators also supplied steam for shellfish boiling. This was an important new service since the cauldrons provided by existing proprietors were often inadequate and put public health at risk. The boilers, steam generators and lift machinery were sensibly housed in the lofty basement, 24 feet high, with groined and vaulted roof.

The hall offered vastly improved selling areas for fish merchants. Once, most dealers crowded into tumbledown sheds. Some lacked even this basic amenity and were obliged to shelter from the elements under large green umbrellas. The crowd milled around and merchants fell prey to pickpockets. Conditions improved somewhat in the 1840s when the salesmen were seated back-to-back at dealing tables, separated laterally by wooden boards for extra security, but this was still unsatisfactory for London's great wholesale fish market. Sir Horace's building provided a massive, high-roofed trading floor, 39,000 sq. ft. in area. This allowed ample space for the neatly regimented rows of salesmen's stands. Fish merchants' shops, with offices above, lined the interior walls of the hall, giving superior business accommodation.

Even in the age before the introduction of refrigeration, the new building offered greater standards of hygiene than its predecessors. The roof was of louvred glass, over 30 feet high, supported by lattice-girders of 60-feet span, giving good interior illumination and ventilation. This helped the market to remain relatively cool, an important requirement with such a highly perishable commodity as fish.

This dignified, ornate edifice, surmounted by the carved stone figure of Britannia, was aptly described by Sir Horace himself:

> The design of the building is Italian in character and the materials used in its construction are Portland stone, with polished grey granite plinths and wall linings and the intervals between the archivolts and windows being filled in with yellow brick facings. The front next Thames Street consists of an arcade

terminated at its eastern and western extremities by pavilion buildings and a pedimented central feature, marking the entrance to the shellfish and dried fish markets. The river front is similar in general treatment but differing in detail.[17]

Relatively late in the market's career, probably in the 1920s, a refrigeration plant and cold store were installed in the basement and a mezzanine floor inserted. The trading floor remained substantially the same, although electric lighting replaced gas and prominent overhead telephones were added as business practices adapted to the pace of the 20th century.

Fish Supplies and Deliveries: Buying and Selling

Billingsgate was famous for the immense variety of both common and exotic fish. Supplies came not only from the United Kingdom fishing ports but also from countries throughout the world. Refrigeration and rapid transport to market helped to make this enormous selection possible. Choice was limited until relatively modern times as fresh fish tended to 'go off' as it was brought slowly to market by sailing vessel or horse-drawn transport. In any case, culinary taste remained fairly conservative. Fewer than 20 varieties of fish were commonly sold at 18th-century Billingsgate. These came from the Thames, the estuary, or nearby coastal ports. Cod was regarded as the most important fish sold. This species was said to be fished by 100 vessels around the coast, each with a crew of eight or nine, making ten trips a year.[18] Haddock, whiting, skate, maid and thornback came from around the coast in general. Mackerel, herring, sprats and pilchards were fished off the shores of Norfolk, Suffolk, Sussex, Devon and Cornwall. Many fish, such as sole, flounders, plaice and dabs, were taken from the Thames estuary.[19]

The Thames itself was an important fishery until river pollution, sewage and effluent from the new industries killed off the fish in the early 19th century. Previously, 400 Thames fishermen, each possessing his own boat. caught 'roach, plaice, smelts, founders, salmon, shad, eels, gudgeon, dace etc.'[20] Salmon was quite plentiful. On one occasion, 10 salmon and 3,000 smelts were taken 'at one haul' in the river towards Wandsworth. Typically, 'fifty thousand smelts were brought daily to Billingsgate and not fewer than three thousand Thames salmon in the season.'[21]

An analysis of the chief fishing ports supplying Billingsgate quoted in Knight's *London* gave a total of over 2,200 vessels from 11 ports. With the exception of Dartmouth in the west, these were concentrated on the coasts of East Anglia, the South and South-East. London provided the greatest single number of fishing vessels, nearly 600, although this total would have included important fishing communities extending eastwards, along the Thames.[22] For example, according to Mayhew, 'The great supply of the staple descriptions of fish to Billingsgate is from the fishermen of Barking in Essex.'[23] Other important suppliers were Yarmouth, Faversham, Rochester and Colchester, each with over 200 vessels. Southampton, Maldon and Dover each had over one hundred.[24]

The fish presented a striking sight on arrival at Billingsgate. 'Some of the heaps of fish would enchant a Dutch painter.'[25] Mayhew was particularly impressed: '... the white bellies of the turbots, strung up bow-fashion, shine like mother-of-pearl, while, the lobsters lying upon them, look intensely scarlet, from the contrast.'[26] 'Curious' fish were few. Occasionally a sturgeon, young shark, or porpoise would be displayed for its novelty. Mayhew actually saw fewer than 20 everyday varieties at Billingsgate. He noted: 'herrings, red herrings, bloaters, soles, sprats, plaice, cod, mackerel, haddock. flounders, eels, mussels, whelk, periwinkles, shrimps, oysters, crabs, lobsters and salmon.'[27]

Many came from home waters. For example, Colchester was noted for oysters and

Leigh for shrimps. Some fish such as sole, plaice and haddock came, in Mayhew's words, from '... coasts within a few hours railway communication of London'.[28] This phrase was not simply a convenient measure of distance but an indication that railway supplies were already having an effect on Billingsgate's trade. Some fish came longer distances – salmon from Scotland, mackerel from the western coast, cod from Doggerbank, the Yorkshire coast, or from Holland and Norway.

Somewhat paradoxically to modern visitors, although Billingsgate was on the bank of the Thames, fish consignments arrived not by sea but by refrigerated container lorry direct from the ports. Originally, all fish arrived at Billingsgate by boat. In the mid-19th century there was competition to unload as vessels, 'square in rigging and somewhat tubby in build', moored in triple tier in the busy Thames off the market.[29]

Although sailing vessels were relatively slow and did not have the benefit of refrigeration, there were ingenious ways of preventing catches from spoiling. The fishing smack proprietors of the important port of Barking gathered ice from the wintry marshes and stored it in ice-houses for use in warmer seasons. According to Mayhew, 'It is sent out in the smacks and the fish is packed in it – such as is not brought alive – to be the better preserved ...'[30] The alternative was to bring the catches of cod alive in welled smacks. The catch was transferred to hatch-covered boats at Gravesend and sent on to Billingsgate. These systems had their disadvantages. Ice was expensive, especially during mild winters, when it had to be imported from Norway. The sailing qualities of the welled smacks were renowned but their catches would deteriorate if contrary winds or calm were encountered.

By the mid-19th century it had become obvious that the problems of supplying London's rapidly increasing population with fish could only be overcome by exploiting the North Sea fishing grounds more effectively and devising faster ways of transporting fish to market. One answer was to adopt the new railway system for deliveries, as already indicated. During the period 1836 to 1874, the majority of London's great railway termini were completed. For the first time, the capital was in effective and rapid communication with provincial towns and cities including the coastal fishing ports. In the 1840s, very early in railway history, a substantial proportion of Billingsgate's supplies were delivered by rail although, even then, the greatest proportion still came from relatively close at hand. 'Fish is now received at Billingsgate from Liverpool, Hull, Bristol, Hartlepool and Durham and from other quarters, which were precluded to it when the means of transport were not sufficiently rapid for so perishable an article. The railways from London the southern coast, especially, have increased the facility of supply.'[31] Mayhew was impressed by the effect of the railways on Billingsgate's trade. Not only had they increased supplies but they had helped to bring down prices.[32] Also the speed of transit meant that fish arrived fresher. Substantially less had to be condemned by the inspectors as unfit for human consumption.[33]

Transportation by rail reached its peak of efficiency a century later. Consignments came long distances from ports in the north of England and Scotland, for example, Hull, Grimsby, Fleetwood and Aberdeen. 'Fish Specials', from distant ports to London, were huge trains sometimes consisting of 40 wagons, carrying as much as 150 tons of fish. A typical journey from Aberdeen to London took 14 hours. To keep fish fresh during transit, the wagons were insulated with felt and kept cool with blocks of dry ice suspended inside. The fish itself was packed in boxes with ice.[34]

Kings Cross became the most important fish terminus, followed by Broad Street. The fish was unloaded at the stations by gangs of railway employees and sent on the last leg of the journey to Billingsgate by railway wagon. These remained horse drawn until well after the introduction of motor vehicles. One observer created a romantic picture of the 5 a.m. arrival of the wagons at Billingsgate, '... just before the hour sounds from the neighbouring steeples, a clatter of hooves and grinding of wheels on the stony road jar through the stillness and a ponderous railway van, heavily burdened, sweeps down Fish Street Hill and pulls up gallantly opposite the yet closed gates of the market.'[35]

The reality was rather different. Not long after Billingsgate gained its improved new market hall, it ironically fell victim to traffic congestion. Railway delivery wagons and fishmongers' vans competed for space in the narrow access roads. Slowly, a system of marshalling Billingsgate traffic and clearing it from the streets before the busy City came to life evolved, although the problem itself was incapable of final solution. There were simply too many vehicles, all arriving at the same time, desperate for space next to the market. In the 1950s, for example, the market traffic absorbed a vast amount of road space from Cannon Street to the Tower. Railway delivery lorries parked in Lower Thames Street, next to the market and in the east part of Monument Street. Fishmongers' vehicles parked in the remaining sections of Lower Thames Street and Monument Street, also Upper Thames Street, Eastcheap and Great Tower Street.[36] Overland transport certainly speeded the fish to Billingsgate but the price to be paid was a mêlée of vehicles when deliveries arrived at the market gates.

3. Steam carriers moored at the quay of Sir Horace Jones' Billingsgate building, around the 1880s.

Despite the railway's early success, it was many years before the market's direct links with the sea were finally severed. Later 19th-century developments of fast steam ships and refrigeration helped to overcome the disadvantages of the slow and inadequate welled sailing smacks. Knight's *London* observed 'the very extraordinary change which has taken place in the supply of salmon for Billingsgate market since it has been brought by steam vessels from Scotland ...'.[37] The most effective use of the steamship, however, proved to be the 'fleeting' system. It was not fishing vessels which delivered to Billingsgate but specialised fast steam carriers 'ferrying' catches from the North Sea. Until the 1930s these carriers were a familiar and evocative sight in the Thames. 'Some time in the night, two steamers, fitted with ice tanks and carrying cargoes from fishing towns along the eastern and north eastern coasts, came up in the Thames and are moored under the flare of the lamps that burn till morning at the back of Billingsgate market'.[38]

In the 1870s most of Billingsgate's fish still came by sea but by the early 1900s rail had overtaken ship. It became apparent that fleeting was uneconomic. Maintenance bills and crews' wages were expensive and coal costs were high. The Grimsby vessels gave up but two Hull companies, the Gamecock and Red Cross fleets, continued after the First World War. Jointly, these fleets sent one carrier daily to Billingsgate. The single carrier proved particularly vulnerable to bad weather and customers lost confidence. A dramatic rise in coal prices finally forced the fleets into voluntary liquidation in 1936. Billingsgate became, in effect, a totally land-locked fish market.[39]

Until the 1950s the relative newcomer, long-distance road haulage, remained uncompetitive. As the 1960s progressed, however, the railways proved increasingly uneconomic compared with road. By the 1970s virtually all supplies arrived at Billingsgate not by rail but by refrigerated container lorry, direct form the ports. As changes in fish deliveries occurred, so market routine became more rationalised.

Billingsgate was unique amongst fish markets, not just for its distinctive personality but because it had evolved into a 'samples market'. Fish consignments were not brought into the building but remained outside in the delivery vehicles, which acted as temporary stores. Only samples were displayed on the merchants' stands.

Buying at Billingsgate was very different in the 19th century, when eels were sold from boats. Mayhew saw 'The Dutch built eel boats with their bulging polished oak sides, half hidden in the river mist'.[40] Their holds were fitted up with long tanks of muddy water containing live eels. 'Wooden sabots and large porcelain pipes are ranged aound the ledges and men in tall fur caps with high cheekbones and rings in their ears, walk the decks.'[41] Customers were rowed out to the vessels by Thames watermen. Under the terms of the 1698 Act, the Dutch enjoyed a concession, probably introduced for political reasons, granting this privilege of selling eels at Billingsgate. The custom survived until the 1930s, when the old boats finally disappeared.

Oyster boats moored alongside Billingsgate Wharf in a long row known as 'Oyster Street', each attended by a salesman in a white apron. Sailors in striped guernseys sat on the boats' sides. 'These holds are filled with oysters – a gray mass of sand and shell – on which is a bushel measure well piled up in the centre, whilst some of them have a blue muddy heap of mussels ...'[42] So great was the demand that buyers crowded the boats, almost causing them to sink.

Wet fish, that is, plaice, sole, fresh haddock, skate, maids, cod and ling, was unloaded from boats, brought into the market in bulk and auctioned. Buyers did not bother with ceremony. 'Round the auction tables stand groups of men turning over the piles of soles and throwing them down, 'til they slide about in their slime: some are smelling them, while others are counting the lots.'[43] 'Doubles' or oblong baskets, tapering to the bottom and containing three to four dozen fish, were piled on wooden forms beneath the auctioneer's rostrum. Then '... a porter catches up a couple of doubles and swings one on each shoulder and the the bids begin'. The salesmen, '... with long account books in their hands, knock down the lots with marvellous rapidity'.[44] These 'Dutch auctions' needed considerable skill, experience and rapid judgement. Buyers shifted rapidly from one salesman to another, single-mindedly demanding only one fact, the price. Salesmen shouted a high figure and the customer promptly countered with a much lower offer. A bargain would be struck as the buyer advanced in price and the seller came down. One observer recalled, 'there is not one of the markets of London which is so little exposed to the chances of collusion or any underhand dealing as that of Billingsgate'.[45]

The Victorian market was a very noisy place. Salesmen stood on their tables, shouting their wares and 'roaring out their prices':

> Ha-a-ansome cod! best in the market! All alive! alive! alive O!
> Ye-o-o! Ye-o-o! here's your fine Yarmouth bloaters!
> Had-had-had-had-haddick! all fresh and good!
> Eels O! Eels O![46]

which combined to make Billingsgate 'a perfect Babel of competition'.

According to Mayhew, fishermen once sold their cargoes direct but in general all fish sent to London was consigned to 'fish factors' or 'Billingsgate salesmen', regarded as men of 'great wealth and influence'. Mayhew counted some 39 principal salesmen specialising in particular types of fish, for example, cod, herring or salmon. There were 80 smaller dealers and as many as 200 shrimp salesmen.[47] In the early 1900s about 200 stands were rented by firms in the market and about 60 fish merchants had premises in the vicinity. They continued to project a well-to-do image: '... along Thames Street, glides a private brougham which stops at the door of one of the crazy, tumbledown old fish shops and a substantial, prosperous looking merchant alights ... You may see him presently, when his shutters are down, disguised in a white smock and cloth cap, writing at his desk among trickling consignments of newly arrived fish ...'[48]

The growth of specialised firms of salesmen, the sending of a substantial proportion of deliveries by rail rather than sea, and the resulting changes in methods of unloading and handling fish inevitably led to the gradual introduction of sale by sample. The main consignments, held back in the delivery vehicles outside, were guaranteed to be the same quality as the fish sample examined by the customer inside the market. 'Nowhere else in the world are the principles of good faith so necessary to trade as at Billingsgate, for selling is done largely by sample.'[49] The procedure had obvious advantages. It was quicker than auctions, reduced unnecessary bulk handling and freed valuable space within the market for more productive use. Seaborne deliveries remained an exception and continued to be auctioned until the final demise of the steam carriers.

Billingsgate's customers included fishmongers, fish fryers, restauranteurs, hoteliers, caterers and buyers from the big stores, not only from London and the West End but also the Home Counties. Even in the 17th century, Billingsgate supplied towns and villages around London with provisions.[50] By the mid-19th century, this regional trade had grown. Mayhew calculated that one-third of Billingsgate's daily fish deliveries were sent into the country.[51]

The majority of customers who bought from the salesmen, however, were of a different class from their 20th-century successors. Only a small proportion were fishmongers. Most were either 'bummarees' or costermongers. A bummeree was a kind of middle man. The derivation of this odd word is uncertain but it probably came from the term 'bum-boat man'. The proprietors of these boats used to purchase stranded fish consignments from wind-bound smacks at Gravesend or the Nore and send the fish overland to Billingsgate by horse, earning a profit for their initiative. Sala was scathing about the bummarees' role. 'The process of bumbareeing is very simple. It consists of buying as largely as your means will afford of an auctioneer, hiring a stall for sixpence and retailing the fish at a swingeing profit.'[52] Mayhew regarded the bummarees as perfectly acceptable businessmen, equivalent to 'a jobber or speculator on the fish exchange.'[53] In effect, bummarees made their living gambling on the uneven fish prices of the era, which could fluctuate by 10 or 20 per cent during a single day's trading. Even Sala admitted that bummarees provided a convenience for small dealers who could not afford to purchase an entire 'double' at auction.

The numbers of bummarees fluctuated but Mayhew says that they were at their greatest from Christmas to the beginning of August, the West End fashionable season. Presumably this resulted in a greater demand for certain types of fish. Many salesmen or fishmongers apparently exploited the situation by 'bummareeing' for a temporary period. It is difficult to say when the practice finally disappeared. One commentator mentions bummarees in the 1930s, buying from wholesale merchants in large quantities and supplying small fishmongers and fryers.[54] Apparently, greater regularity of supplies and the end of fish auctions removed the opportunity to speculate. It also became easier for customers to buy small quantities of fish without the need for a middleman.

The largest single class of customer at Billingsgate was the costermonger, who sold fish from carts in the working class districts of the city. The market's busiest time for costermongers was 7 a.m. on a Friday morning, after the regular bummarees and fishmongers had departed. Fridays were special, for religious reasons. Many families, especially Roman Catholics, made fish their main meal on that day. On reaching the Monument '... as you walk along, a fresh line of costers' barrows are creeping in or being backed into almost impossible openings ...'.[55]

Mayhew felt that the combination of rail deliveries to Billingsgate which brought down the price of fish and the industry of the costermongers, had helped to change the diet of London's working classes. 'This cheap food, through the agency of the costermongers, is conveyed to every poor man's door, both in the thickly-crowded streets where the poor reside – a family at least in a room – in the vicinity of Drury-lane and of Whitechapel, in Westminster, Bethnal-green and St Giles and through the long miles of the suburbs.'[56] This trade was enormous – one-third of Billingsgate's supplies were purchased by the costermongers. The principal staple of the 'street fishmonger' was sole, which had the advantage of being in supply virtually all the year round. Herrings, mackerel, whiting, Dutch eels and plaice were also popular varieties. Mayhew estimated that as much as 116,000 tons of wet fish were purchased annually on the streets of London, of which the bulk, five-sixths, was herrings.[57] Again, it is difficult to say when the costers finally abandoned Billingsgate. They remained a common sight earlier this century, when, as trade peaked and turned at 6.30 a.m., '... the costers who have been clustering their barrows at the lower end of Love Lane, are swooping in to bargain and buy.'[58]

There was another kind of buyer, the fish fryer. Modern 'fish and chips' were not introduced until the late 1860s[59] but fried fish was sold in the streets before that date. Modern fryers often preferred the slightly cheaper but still high quality fish from the Billingsgate cold store. Their 19th-century predecessors bought 'offal', pieces of broken, mixed fish, but still fresh. In words notable for the choice of vocabulary, Sala referred to a dealer from Somers Town who regularly bought from 15 to 20 doubles of offal. 'To him resort to purchase stock those innumerable purveyors of fried fish who make our courts and bye-streets redolent with the oleaginous perfumes of their hissing cauldrons.'[60]

The total fish tonnages handled at Billingsgate were impressive. Mayhew marvelled at the sheer quantities. In 1848, the first year for which figures are readily available, about 2,100 tons of fish arrived weekly at Billingsgate.[61] The underlying trend was for tonnages to rise, in parallel with greater demand, as London's population continued to multiply. In the peak year of 1910, a gargantuan weekly average of about 3,800 tons was delivered to the market.[62] Two World Wars and periods of economic slump and austerity adversely affected trade. Totals did not recover until the late 1940s.

Although Britain enjoyed unprecedented prosperity in the 1950s, this was not directly reflected in an increase in Billingsgate's tonnages. In fact, weekly totals declined. The reasons were manifold. More fish was received headless or filleted, so that the same amount actually weighed less. The nation's dietary habits changed and there was a reduction in fish consumption. People changed to newly-available frozen and convenience foods. Instead of being sent fresh to Billingsgate, a large proportion of catches was bought at the ports by food companies for the manufacture of the ever-popular frozen fish fingers.

Nevertheless, at the time of Billingsgate's closure and removal to the new site, fish merchants were encouraged by increased sales, contrary to the national trend. In 1982, weekly averages of 1,500 tons of fish were recorded. The rise was explained by the demand from the capital's new ethnic population who regarded fish as an important part of the daily diet. Another factor was a generally greater 'health awareness', especially in sophisticated London and the Home Counties, which persuaded people to eat more fish.

In any case, Billingsgate prided itself not so much on volume but service, quality and unparalleled variety. The choice was indeed spectacular. Twenty ports in Britain, from Aberdeen to Brixham, from Hastings, Rye and Lowestoft to Hull, Grimsby and Peterhead, sent fish catches daily. Further supplies came from 29 countries worldwide, from Canada to Brazil, Japan to New Zealand, Greenland to Spain. Catches were sent long distances speedily by air freight. Vans brought fish from Heathrow to Billingsgate. Over 100 types of fish were available, ranging from traditional staples such as cod, sole, plaice and haddock, to 'exotics' like cuckoo wrasse, cuttlefish, swordfish, bonito and squid.[63]

Billingsgate Porters

However fish arrived at Billingsgate, by sea, rail, road or air, porters were always needed to unload the consignments. Similarly, whether deliveries were sold by auction or sample, porters were vital to carry fish into the market, or to customers' premises or vehicles. Without porters to undertake the backbreaking work of shifting heavy burdens, Billingsgate could not have functioned effectively.

There were about 240 porters at Billingsgate, individually licensed by the City Corporation and belonging to the Transport and General Workers Union. Their first task, at 5 a.m. each day, was to move fish samples from the delivery vehicles in the lorry park to the merchants' stands on the trading floor. The job was called 'shoring in', a term derived from the old practice of carrying fish ashore from the fishing vessels which once called at Billingsgate wharf. The porters' second role was to deliver the fish from the supply lorry to the customer's van. This job was referred to as 'barrowing', for obvious reasons, and could involve a round trip along Lower Thames Street as far as Custom

4.   An amazing traffic jam in front of the market, 1937. On the left is Lower Thames Street, looking east, and on the right, Monument Street. The triangular building is the Haddock Market of 1888 (demolished 1971). The modern Peninsular House and Republic National Bank of New York now occupy the site. Most delivery vehicles were still horse-drawn but a few petrol-driven lorries are discernible.

House, with a heavily-laden hand barrow. Salesmen paid the porters' wages. Customers paid an additional sum, known as 'bobbin money', for each purchase delivered. Far more porters, about 1,500, were hired in the 1930s, when they could earn £8 weekly and 2d. a stone bobbin money.[64] This term was derived from the unique bobbin hats once universally worn by the porters.

Few modern porters still wore these curious hats of tarred wood and leather, although they were in common use until the 1950s. One authority mentions that this headgear was copied from the helmets worn by bowmen at the battle of Agincourt.[65] Bobbin hats were eminently functional. The flat crown enabled fish boxes to be balanced on the head, an essential technique in a crowded market. It was also quite a feat when fish boxes weighed eight stone and still a formidable undertaking even with modern packaging, which reduced boxes to about three stone in weight. The turned-up brim protected the wearer from the runnels of melting ice and fish slime which trickled from the boxes. These hats could be purchased from a long-vanished shop in Love Lane for the sum of 30 shillings. It is surprising that Mayhew made no mention of this distinctive headgear in his meticulous description of Billingsgate. The casual porters or 'bobbers' of his day may possibly have lent their name to the terms 'bobbin hat' and 'bobbin money'.

In Mayhew's time, some women were still working, although their numbers had substantially declined in the preceding 30 years. He saw '... women, with long limp tails of codfish dangling from their aprons, elbow their way through the crowd'.[66] Then known as 'fish fags', they were the working descendants of the fishwives who mocked Ned Ward.

The majority of the heavy work, however, was performed by authorised labourers who were still organised into medieval trade societies, controlled by the City Corporation. Joining was not easy. Numbers were strictly limited and stringent conditions had to be fulfilled. Above all, it was necessary to become a Freeman of the City, for which a residence qualification and an enrolment fee were essential. There were two classes of authorised labourers. fellowship porters and ticket porters. Both were granted certain privileges, although these were not clearly defined and there were frequent conflicts, sometimes violent, between the two branches.

Nominally, fellowship porters enjoyed the exclusive right '... of carrying from the ship to market all fish or shellfish, sold by the tale [number] or·by measure; thus oysters, mussels, sprats etc can only be portered from the water, legally, by him ...'[67] These porters had to provide their own baskets, if necessary, and were allowed to charge 2d. a bushel for moving shellfish. Mayhew observed as '... a tall porter, with a black oyster bag, staggers past, trembling under the weight of his load, his back and shouders wet with drippings from the sack. "Shove on one side!" he mutters from between his clenched teeth as he forces his way through the mob.'[68] The numbers were seasonal, varying from 40 to one hundred. The second branch of authorised labourers, the ticket porters, had somewhat different duties. They had the exclusive right of carrying dried fish such as red herring or bloaters. Their fee was 1½d. a box. About 40 men were engaged in this work.

There were, in addition, about 400 unprivileged porters, 'foreigners', 'bobbers' and 'roughs'. Their duties varied but were strictly limited in scope. Foreigners, so called because, as porters they were not Freemen, were paid by the fish merchants to receive the fish brought by the fellowship porters from the ships. Bobbers were sent from the market with goods to purchasers nearby, particularly retailers buying small quantities. Roughs were casual labourers who undertook any job, often helping railway staff unload the railway delivery wagons.

With their archaic restrictive practices, the fellowship and ticket porters became an inconvenient embarrassment to the Corporation. Jealous of their traditions, they would not adapt their practices to life in a modern market. The City refused to protect their ancient privileges and closed the membership lists. Long before the turn of the century, they had been replaced by the licensed porters who were a familiar sight at Billingsgate until it closed. Details of the porters' routine and mannerisms were favourite subjects for Billingsgate commentators. For example, Knight's *London* described the ritual of the 5 a.m. start to the day.

> At the lower end of the market, nearest the boats, porters stand with baskets of fish on their heads. Not one of them is allowed to have the advantage over his fellows by an unfair start, or to overstep the line marked out by the clerk of the Market. The instant the clock strikes the race commences and each porter rushes at his utmost to the respective salesman to whom his burden is consigned.[69]

Once, porters had to clamber up steps from the vessels with their heavy loads. Later, a bridge attached to a floating pontoon made the task easier, although still dangerous if a man were unfortunate enough to slip. 'A broad iron bridge slopes down to them and down one side of the bridge porters are hurrying empty-handed and up the other side, porters stream one after the other with boxes on their heads'.[70] Ironically, in the 1920s, shortly before ship deliveries ceased entirely, this danger was removed when an electric conveyor was installed to shift the boxes direct from steam carriers to market.

On land, porters gave the impression of frantic activity. The moment 5 a.m. struck, 'fish porters innumerable hurtle as it were from the clouds and up from the earth, as if every paving stone were a trap door and swarming everywhere in white smocks and round iron hard hats'.[71] Loads were carried quickly with 'characteristically head-erect spring-heeled step'[72] normally without pausing once underway. Despite the improvements, it was always heavy work. Good balance, sure footedness, strength and stamina were essential. A sense of humour helped.

Billingsgate's Closure

Billingsgate's cramped site and old buildings made effective modernisation impossible. This area gave the powerful impression that a part of Victorian London had somehow survived amongst the late 20th-century office blocks.

Billingsgate became so indispensable that, despite its shortcomings, it defeated successive attempts to establish rival markets. In 1830, the short-lived wholesale fish-market for Westminster, at Hungerford Market, failed to attract business.[73] Even the later well-equipped and advantageously-sited Shadwell Fish Market, opened in 1885, proved unappealing to the trade compared with Billingsgate.[74] Until the late 20th century, Billingsgate refused to move and remained an isolated fish-trading outpost in a City increasingly specialising in finance. Billingsgate was living evidence of the well-known geographers' maxim that '... no human settlement is more difficult to supplant than an established market'.[75]

The end came only when, in effect, the market was cut in two and mortally wounded by the improvement of Lower Thames Street to take a greater volume of traffic. Market vehicles were faced with insuperable parking problems. Porters risked life and limb every time they rushed a heavy, stubborn barrow across the street. The building itself was separated from much of its business by a moving steel barrier of trucks and cars. It was reluctantly accepted that Billingsgate was no longer viable. Plans were finalised during 1981 for the move to a new market building on the north quay of the West India Dock, in the Borough of Tower Hamlets. On Saturday 16 January 1982 Billingsgate finally closed, bringing to an end a trading tradition on the old site that had endured since Saxon times.

In the course of preparing for the inevitable, a great deal of sadness and nostalgia was evident amongst Billingsgate's workers. Perhaps this mood helps to explain the origins of an intriguing prophecy then current. It was predicted that when the antiquated, badly-insulated coldstore was switched off, the frozen subsoil beneath would melt and bring the edifice crashing down. Whether there was substance in the rumour was debatable but, needless to say, Sir Horace Jones' robust design survived without a tremor to become listed as a Grade II Historic Monument.

However, the place was not the same. Gone was the busy hubbub on the trading floor, the jostling, shouting crowds of salesmen and customers, the grating sounds of the iron-shod wheels of the porters' barrows on granite sets, the warning cries of 'mind yer backs!', the silvery, glistening sides of fish and the characteristically overpowering odour of Billingsgate's stock in trade.

References

1. *A Survey of London*, J. Stow. Reprinted from text of 1603. Editor C.K. Kingsford, 1908.
2. J. Strype's enlarged edition of Stow's *Survey*, 1720, quotes payment of tolls at Billingsgate in 1016, 'inter Leges Ethelredi'.
3. Evidence of Roman occupation was excavated from a site immediately to the west. Department of Urban Archaeology, Museum of London, 1982.
4. *London*, ed. C. Knight, Vol.IV. Revised by E. Walford 1857-77, based largely on 1842 edition.
5. 'The Customs of Billyngesgate', *Liber Albus: The White Book of the City of London*, compiled by John Carpenter and Richard Whittington, 1419. Quoted from 'Billingsgate: a Central Metropolitan Market', J.H. Bird, *Geographical Journal*, Vol. 124, 1958.
6. The western part of Thames Street was renamed Upper Thames Street. The eastern part, below London Bridge, was renamed Lower Thames Street. Billingsgate Market was on the south side of this portion.
7. J. Stow, op. cit.
8. Ibid.
9. 'An Act for Making Billingsgate a Free Market for the Sale of Fish'. 10 W. III c. 13, 1698. Quoted from J.H. Bird, op. cit. Modern Billingsgate closed not only on Sundays, but on Mondays too.
10. *The London Spy*, Ned Ward (1667-1731). Ed. A.L. Hayward, 1927.
11. Ned Ward, op. cit.
12. C. Knight, op. cit.
13. *Twice round the clock; or the hours of the day and night in London*, G.A.H. Sala, 1859.
14. *London Labour and the London Poor*, 'The London Street Folk', Vol. I, H. Mayhew, 1861. (Included material originally gathered 1849-50.)
15. J.H. Bunning was architect of another notable building in the vicinity, the Coal Exchange, Lower Thames Street (1847-9, demolished *c.*1961). This building was evidence of Billingsgate's former association with the coal trade.
16. Quoted from published remarks of Sir Horace Jones.
17. 'A Short Notice of the Metropolitan Markets', Sir Horace Jones. *Transactions of the Royal Institute of British Architects*, 1877-78. Sir Horace designed other famous buildings, including Smithfield Meat Market and Tower Bridge.
18. 'Fish Marketing in London in the first half of the Eighteenth Century', W.M. Stern, from *Trade, Government and Economy in Pre-Industrial England*. Essays presented to F.J. Fisher, 1976.
19. Ibid.
20. C. Knight, op. cit.
21. Ibid.
22. Ibid.
23. *The Morning Chronicle Survey of Labour and the Poor*, The Metropolitan Districts, Vol. VI, H. Mayhew. Published 1982 with introduction by Peter Razzell. The original material was gathered 1849-50.
24. C. Knight, op. cit.
25. Ibid.
26. H. Mayhew, op. cit., 1861.
27. H. Mayhew, op. cit., 1982.
28. Ibid.
29. G.A.H. Sala, op. cit.
30. H. Mayhew, op. cit., 1982.
31. C. Knight, op. cit.
32. H.Mayhew, op. cit., 1861.
33. H. Mayhew, op. cit., 1982.
34. J.H. Bird, op. cit.
35. 'Round London's Big Markets', A. Rutland, from *Living London*, ed. G.R. Sims 1902.
36. J.H. Bird, op. cit.
37. C. Knight, op. cit.
38. G.R. Sims, op. cit.
39. *The Fishing News*, 7 March 1936 and 14 March 1936. I am grateful to P. O'Driscoll for these references to the end of the steam carrier fleets.
40. H. Mayhew, op. cit., 1861.
41. Ibid.

42. Ibid.
43. Ibid.
44. G.A.H. Sala, op. cit.
45. C. Knight, op. cit.
46. H. Mayhew, op. cit., 1861.
47. H. Mayhew, op. cit., 1982.
48. G.R. Sims, op. cit.
49. *London's Markets*, W.J. Massingham, *c.* 1930.
50. J. Stow, op. cit.
51. H. Mayhew, op. cit., 1982.
52. G.A.H. Sala, op. cit. Note his version of the term was 'bumbaree'.
53. H. Mayhew, op. cit., 1861.
54. W.J. Massingham, op. cit.
55. H. Mayhew, op. cit., 1861.
56. Ibid.
57. Ibid.
58. G.R. Sims, op. cit.
59. L.B.C. Radio broadcast, '121st Anniversary of Fish and Chips', *A M* 29.8.88.
60. G.A.H. Sala, op. cit.
61. Derived from figures in J.H. Bird, op. cit.
62. Ibid.
63. 'The Wonderful World of Fish', National Federation of Fishmongers Ltd. Trade Exhibition and National Fishmongers' Craftsmanship Competition 1980. Souvenir programme compiled by D.W. Bradfield.
64. 'Billingsgate', *Picture Post*, 22 April 1939.
65. *The London Encyclopaedia*, ed. B. Weinreb and C. Hibbert, 1981.
66. H. Mayhew, op. cit., 1861. Note use of 'tale', not 'tail'.
67. H. Mayhew, op. cit., 1982.
68. H. Mayhew, op. cit., 1861.
69. C. Knight, op. cit.
70. G.R. Sims, op. cit.
71. Ibid.
72. J.H. Bird, op. cit.
73. C. Knight, op. cit. An Act for establishing a fish-market in Westminster was passed in 1749, but not implemented until 1830. It failed because dues were very heavy and dealers found they could easily go to the more amply-supplied Billingsgate once they had got into their carts.
74. Report of Common Council Meeting, 23 July 1908. Guildhall Library. Also 'Billingsgate versus Shadwell', *Fishing News*, P. O'Driscoll, 26 February 1982. The Shadwell Market site was purchased by the L.C.C. in 1910, and it was redeveloped as the King Edward VII Memorial Park, just below the main entrance to London Dock.
75. Sir Halford Mackinder, quoted from J.H. Bird, op. cit.

The photographs in this book were taken by John Edwards, formerly of the Museum of London's Photographic Department, during a two year period from 1980 to 1981, as part of a museum project to record the appearance and working life of old Billingsgate. A decision was made at the outset to film in black and white. This suited the subdued colours and dim light of the scene. With black and white film, it was usually possible to dispense with flash, even though light levels were low. Natural light was used whenever possible in order to achieve greater spontaneity and to capture authentically the market's distinctive atmosphere. The majority of exposures were taken with a hand-held 35mm SLR camera in order effectively to record the action in crowded and confined spaces. On certain occasions, a wide-angle or zoom lens was used, for example, the high-level pictures of the trading floor. For the architectural studies, a larger format camera was adopted. Over 1,500 photographs were taken on a regular series of visits. The following selection is both a comprehensive illustration of the busy working market and an evocation of a vanished aspect of London's rich and varied history, bygone Billingsgate.

Bibliography

Official publications held by Guildhall Library
Billingsgate Market Acts of 1698, 1846 and 1871
Corporation of London, *Report of Common Council Meeting*, 23.7.1908, 'closure of Shadwell Market' (1908)
Corporation of London, *Bye-laws, Rules, Orders and Regulations for Billingsgate Market 1876-1936* (1936)
Corporation of London, *Billingsgate Market: The World's Premier Fish Market* (*c*.1968)

Printed Books
Business Archives Council, *Billingsgate Market: Survey of the Archives* (1981)
Forshaw, A. and Bergström, T., *Markets of London* (1983)
Knight, C. (ed.), *London*, vol. IV (1842), revised E. Walford (1875-1877)
Massingham, W.J., *London's Markets* (*c*.1930)
Mayhew, H., *London Labour and the London Poor*, 'The London Street Folk', vol. I (1861)
Mayhew, H., *The Morning Chronicle Survey of Labour and the Poor* (The Metropolitan Districts), vol. VI, intro-
    duction by P. Razzell (1982)
Morgan, K.O. (ed.), *The Oxford Illustrated History of Britain* (1984)
Oakey, C., *Billingsgate from within*, 'An account of the work carried on at the Mission and Dispensary' (*c*.1935)
Rutland, A., *Living London*, 'Round London's Big Markets', ed. G.R. Sims (1902)
Sala, G.A.H., *Twice round the clock; or the hours of the day and night in London* (1859)
Stern, W.M., *The Porters of London* (1960)
Stern, W.M., *Trade, Government and Economy in Pre-Industrial England*, 'Fish Marketing in London in the first half
    of the Eighteenth Century'. Essays presented to F.J. Fisher (1976)
Stow, J., *A Survey of London*, reprinted from text of 1603, ed. C.L. Kingsford (1908)
Stow, J., *A Survey of London*, 1603, 'corrected, improved and very much enlarged', J. Strype (1720)
Ward, Ned, *The London Spy* (1667-1731), ed. A.L. Hayward (1927)

Journals
Bird, J.H., *Geographical Journal*, vol. 124, 'Billingsgate: a Central Metropolitan Market' (1958)
Jones, Sir Horace, *Transaction of the Royal Institute of British Architects*, 'A short Notice of the Metropolitan
    Markets' (1877-1878)

Newspapers amd periodicals, trade and professional publications
Bradfield, D.W., *The Wonderful World of Fish*, souvenir programme, Trade Exhibition and National Fish-
    mongers' Craftsmanship Competition (1980)
Country Life, 'Billingsgate' (1.9.1928)
The Chiel', *The Fish Trade Gazette*, 'Billingsgate Today' (20.3.1915)
The Fishing News, various articles on steam carriers (7.3.1936 and 14.3.1936)
Hannan, B., *Fishing News*, 'Billingsgate' (5.2.1982)
Horwell, V., *The Guardian*, 'Tails of the South Pacific' (30.7.1988)
O'Driscoll, P., *Fishing News*, a four-part article on Billingsgate:
'Roman Legend to Victorian Sewer' (5.2.1982)
'Billingsgate Must Go!' (12.2.1982)
'Billingsgate versus Shadwell' (26.2.1982)
'The Last Bell' (5.3.1982)
Picture Post, 'Billingsgate' (28.4.1939)
Tabor, C.J., *The Fish Trade Gazette*, 'The History of Billingsgate' (20.3.1915)
Walker, I., *Observer*, 'Melt-Down at Billingsgate' (17.1.1982)
The Worshipful Company of Fishmongers, *Short History* (*c*.1973)

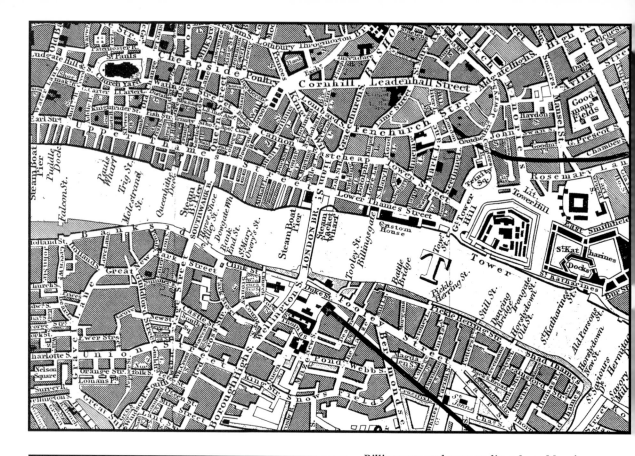

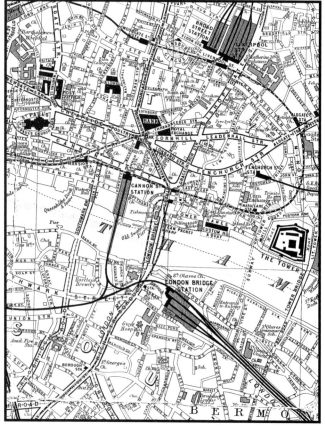

Billingsgate and surroundings from Mogg's 'London and its Environs', *c.*1850. (*Reproduced by permission of the Museum of London.*)

Billingsgate and surroundings from Bartholomew's 'New Plan of London', *c.*1895. (*Reproduced by permission of the Museum of London.*)

The Plates

5. Early morning darkness at Billingsgate Market, showing heavy congestion in Lower Thames Street. Through-traffic was temporarily diverted to allow market vehicles to park. The Tower of London can be seen in the distance.

Billingsgate Market
Building

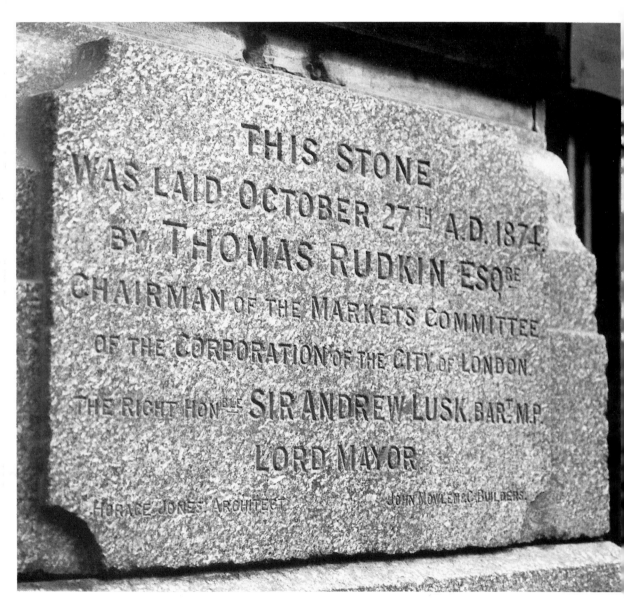

6.   Foundation stone, Lower Thames Street frontage.

7. Porters rest a fish barrow at the same spot. Only the modern packaging reveals the very recent date of the photograph.

8. Main entrance, Lower Thames Street, surmounted by the central pedimented feature of Britannia, appropriately flanked by carved dolphins.

9.   The complete frontage, including the north-east (left) and north-west (right) corner pavilions. The building has since been renovated, converted and refurbished for future use as a banking hall.

10.   The building from the north-east, showing the corner premises of Baxter & Son Ltd., Wholesale Fish Merchants, No. 16 Billingsgate Market. In the foreground can be seen the wide expanse of Lower Thames Street.

11. Billingsgate Market from the River Thames showing the lorry park (left) and the colonnaded frontage of Custom House (right). The modern rectangular buildings on the quayside have since been demolished. In the background, the river terrace, climbed by a maze of narrow lanes and alleys including Lovat Lane and St Mary-at-Hill, rises steeply to Eastcheap.

12. Old Billingsgate Quay from the north bank of the Thames. near Custom House. Ships once unloaded fish catches here. In the background, early morning commuters stream across London Bridge.

13. The sharply pitched, tiled rooftops of Billingsgate, overlooked by the distinguished column of the Monument (left) and the newly completed National Westminster Tower (centre right).

14. The distinctive silhouette of one of Billingsgate's famous rooftop dolphin weathervanes.

Interior Features:
Shops & Offices

15. Shellfish and eel sundries.

16. Baxter & Son Ltd., in the east wall. As the big enamel sign indicated, the firm specialised in shellfish and once handled the largest proportion entering the market.

17. One of the arcades near Baxters, ornamented with appropriate designs of fish in wrought iron.

18. The interior of Thompson & Lewellen, 'Sundriesmen to the Fish Trade', who had been at Billingsgate for over 200 years.

19. Brightly illuminated shops on the east wall, including Smithers & Skinner Ltd. and John Koch Ltd., 14 and 13 Billingsgate Market respectively.

20. Eastern wall of the trading floor, looking towards Lower Thames Street, showing the well-known premises of Thompson & Lewellen, 11 Billingsgate Market. Note the tall columns supporting the wide lattice girders carrying the glass louvred roof.

21. Smithers & Skinner, 'For all kinds of wet fish', showing the cold box and cast-iron spiral staircase to the upper offices. This layout was typical of the fish merchants' shops built into the market walls.

22. Upper offices at Smithers & Skinner, specialists in Norwegian farm salmon, 'Mowi Brand' and Norwegian Peeled Prawns.

23. Western area of the trading floor, thoroughly hosed down after the day's trading. The complete area will be used as a banker's dealing floor after conversion.

24. Western wall of the trading floor, showing L. and D. Hart, 7 Billingsgate Market, shellfish specialists. Most fish merchants were long-established family firms, often dating back to the last century.

25. An unusual view upwards from the trading floor, revealing the intricate tracery of wooden beams and trusses supporting the roof.

CAUTION
Wet
floors

CAUTION
Keep
gangway
clear

26. It was more sensible to keep an eye on the floor, a slippery hazard to the unwary.

The Corridor

27. View along the old wooden corridor on the first floor of Billingsgate Market. The Toll Office was on the left and the office of P.F. Farmer Ltd. on the right.

28. Mr. Old, Toll Inspector, compiling details of fish deliveries in his corridor office after the morning's trade. Figures were submitted to the Superintendent's Office.

29. Office of P.F. Farmer Ltd., wholesale fish salesmen, 22 The Corridor.

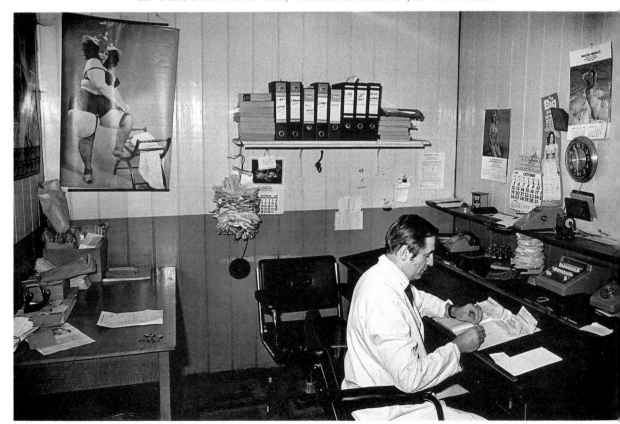

30. The door to the General Office on the first floor. Billingsgate traders belonged to the London Fish Merchants' Association, which set rules of conduct. The Association owned a fleet of 19 lorries which supplied the market through the night with fish deliveries from Hemming Street depot, Bethnal Green.

31. Old glass door, General Office. The London Wholesale Fish Trade organised bulk fish delivery schemes, road transport and information on coastal supplies.

32. Interesting detail at the end of The Corridor, showing the louvred glass panes of the roof. The Corridor, part of Sir Horace Jones' original design, was intended as a haddock market but was replaced by the building opposite Billingsgate, constructed in 1888 for this purpose.

Management

BILLINGSGATE MARKET

OFFICES

OFFICES	
FIRST	**2ND FLOOR**
FLOOR	
SUPERINTENDENT'S	
FISHMETERS, FISHMONGERS COMPANY	44B B.H.WITT
LONDON FISH TRADE ASSOCIATION	47. BOWEN & SIMMOND
2 LUXTON & Cº	G. TRINGHAM LTD. 48
4/7 F.G. JARY LTD	
21/22 SYDNEY JACOBS & SON	
H & J. DELMONTE Nº 27	
28 J & A. WALTERS	
36 G. F. HUNT	

33. Old Billingsgate office indicator, Lower Thames Street entrance, painted with the arms of the City of London which owned the market.

34. 'Finger sign' to the Superintendent's Offices.

35. Mr. Butcher, Billingsgate Superintendent, in his first floor office. He was responsible for day-to-day management, assisted by about 50 clerical, engineering, cleansing and maintenance staff.

A Morning's Trade

Panoramic early morning views of the eastern half of the trading floor, taken during a single four-hour period from John Koch's offices, reveal the characteristic ebb and flow of trade.

42. 5.50 a.m. Lights on. A quiet moment before the mass of customers arrives. Many samples were already in place at the stands on the spotlessly clean floor.

43. 7.40 a.m. Business brisk, debris accumulating on the floor, '... a pandemonium of ordered disorder, a welter of slush, iced water and slime that penetrates and clings ...'. In the foreground, from left to right, are the stands of Micks Eel Supply, Bowen & Simmons, and Fame Foods.

44. 9.55 a.m. Lights off, business over. Tidying the litter and hosing the floor were now priorities.

45. 10.00 a.m. Shutters down, market closed.

Business on the Stands

46. Micks Eel Supply, 7.00 a.m.

47. Live eels were stored for sale in large, steel-drawered cabinets.

48. Home-made sign at eelstand.

49. Porter delivers fish boxes to Fame Foods. Under the byelaws, stands were limited to a 7ft. frontage and 7ft. 6ins. depth.

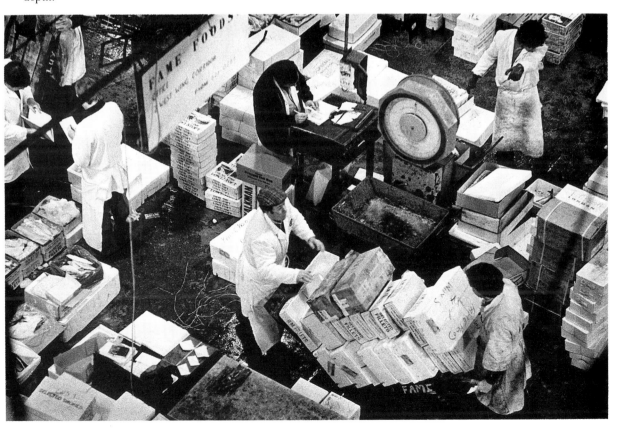

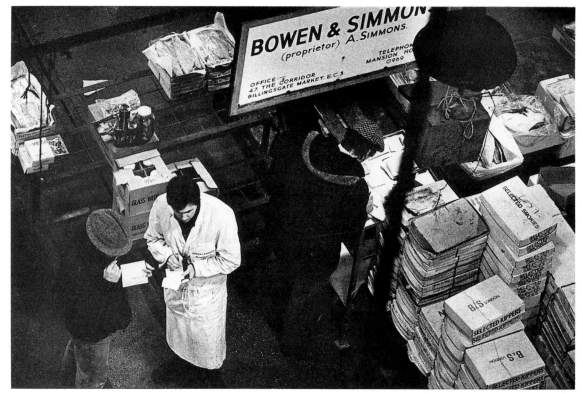

50. A white-coated salesman enters accounts beside stacked boxes of kippers on the Bowen & Simmons stand.

51. A customer reaches to make thorough inspection of a herring sample, watched by salesman, notebook in hand!

52. Completing accounts books over kipper samples.

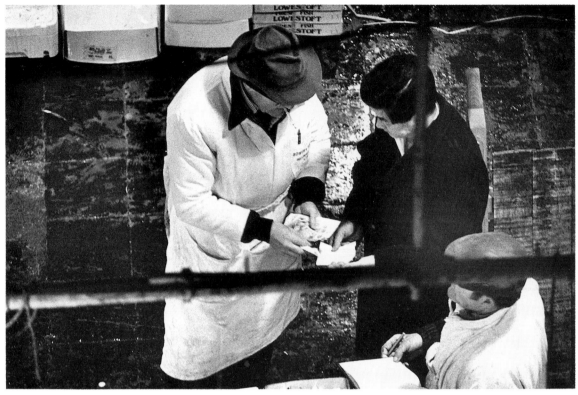

53 A customer pays the salesman. The pound coin had not then been introduced.

54. A porter and salesman enter their accounts. Porters wore a smock and coarse apron, whereas salesmen wore a white coat, three-pocket apron and leggings.

On the Trading Floor

55. Customers around a busy stand.

56. A purchase completed.

57. A shark, too big for the standard box, is kept chilled in crushed ice from the Billingsgate Cold Store.

58. A smartly-dressed customer, sensibly attired for the occasion in wellingtons, is attended by a salesman at his desk.

59. Official notice. The market was open to the trade from 5.00 a.m. to 10.00 a.m., five days a week, closing Sundays and Mondays.

BILLINGSGATE MARKET

MEMBERS OF THE TRADE ONLY SERVED

MER, 01-283 5362

P.G.OVERY

P.G.OVERY

P.G.OVERY

DOUBLE FF

JAMES NASH & SON LTᴰ

REGᵈ OFFICES: 3ᵃ ᴄ 3ᴬ WEST WING

60. About 90 firms rented stands such as this.

REN & BARROW L.

127 LOWER THAMES Sᵗ. E.C.3

BILLINGSGATE
CLOSED

61. A customer pauses to consider.

62. A customer indicates his purchase.

01– 626 2163		
SMOKED SALMON		
	Best	**Imp.**
Whole Sides from	3·80	2·60
Fully Trimmed "	4·50	2·90
Pre-Sliced "	5·20	3·35
Sliced Vac.Pak "	6·70	4·70
Grav Laks "	4·40	2·20
Paté		1·35
Smoked Eel Fillets		2·20
" Mackerel "		0·60
Cocktail 's s'		1·50
.ALL PRICES PER POUND		

63. Smoked salmon prices.

64. A porter returns empty boxes past a salesman busy on the telephone.

65. A salesman at one of the typical old sloping topped desks.

66. A porter arrives with more fish samples. Because of the narrow gangways, byelaws limited market barrows and trolleys to 2ft. 4ins. width and not more than two wheels.

67. An old desk, humorously decorated with a Disney character and amply provided with telephones.

68. A salesman takes a 'quick stretch' just outside the market.

69. A purchase in progress at A.H. Cox (Billingsgate) Ltd., 'Fish Factors and Commission Agents', with the distinctive address of No. 1 Billingsgate Market, facing Lower Thames Street, at the north-west corner.

Billingsgate Lorry Park

70. The lorry park, adjacent to the west wall of the market, overlooked by the Monument. A focus of activity, where delivery vehicles parked for unloading. Porters 'shored in' or 'barrowed' fish to merchants' stands or customers' vans.

71. Toll Inspector checks a fish delivery. 'Driver's notes' gave the details. The official toll was £1.20 per ton, sometimes collected on the spot but usually dealt with by correspondence.

72. Porters unloading fish boxes. The lorry park was acquired in 1940 to relieve parking pressures in Lower Thames Street. It is now occupied by the blue glass bulk of the new Midland Montagu building.

73. Fishmeter on his rounds, inspecting a consignment.

74. The tea stall was popular with porters, who sometimes treated local vagrants.

75. Tea stall counter.

76. Vagrants congregated in the lorry park, attracted by the prospect of casual employment.

77. A vagrant helps a porter across Lower Thames Street.

78. A vagrant suspicious of the camera. Porters sometimes hired these men, whom they called 'scats' or, more politely, 'pusher uppers'.

Porter's Work

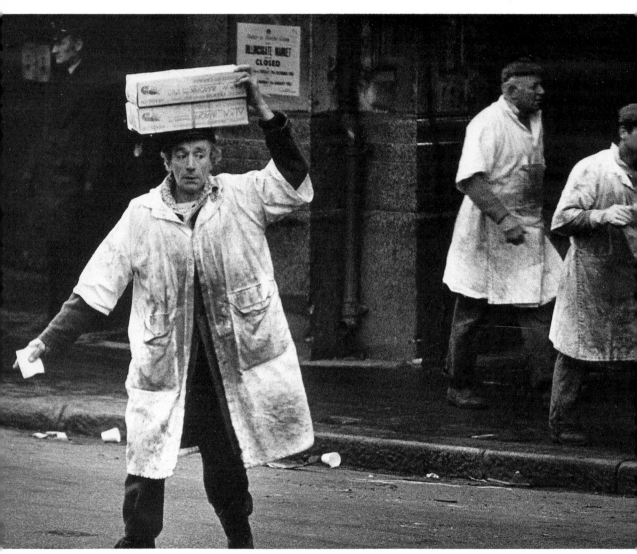

79. Keeping a wary eye on the traffic, a porter crosses Lower Thames Street, fish boxes on head and slip in hand. Slips recorded details of purchases and were passed to porters by the merchants for presentation at the delivery vehicle.

80. Destination board at a merchant's stand. Many retailers' vehicles were parked at Custom House, east of the market.

81. Porters deliver purchases to retailers' lorries parked at St Dunstan in the East, opposite Custom House. The site on the left is the east wall of the present Trustee Savings Bank building.

82. Porters arriving at Custom House.

83. A porter unloads his barrow into a customer's van.

84. A porter balances fish boxes on the crown of his traditional but still functional bobbin hat, apparently effortlessly.

85. The scene at Custom House in early morning darkness.

86. Porter and pusher upper, Monument Street. *The Walrus* public house remains but the other premises in the background have either been converted or replaced with offices.

87. A job for a pusher upper.

88. Pushing up towards the Monument.

89. The three methods commonly used by porters; trolley, balancing or barrow.

90. Porters approach the Monument.

91. At the other side of the Monument another kind of worker, early commuters, cut across the Western end of Monument Street en route to the office.

92. A convoy of porters return their empty trolleys from the Monument.

93. A really heavy load.

94. Porters briefly rest their barrows in front of the market.

95. A reminder to porters.

96. A container lorry is unloaded directly in front of the market.

97. A cheerful porter loads his trolley.

Hazards of Old Billingsgate!
Lower Thames Street

98. A porter calmly dodges in front of a coach.

99. A porter rushes his overloaded trolley across the path of a heavy lorry. An illustration of why the market had to move.

100. Body bent with effort, a porter negotiates the traffic.

101. Aware of the speeding cars, a porter safely crosses Lower Thames Street.

102. A chaotic mixture of porters, market vehicles and through traffic.

103. A view showing the temporary diversion of westbound traffic away from the market front and parked retailers' vehicles. These had to be cleared by 9.00 a.m. to avoid unnecessary hold ups.

A Billingsgate Veteran

104. An elderly porter
begins the tricky crossing of
Lower Thames Street.

105. The porter receives a
protective helping hand as
he crosses the traffic's path.

106. A couple of pusher uppers give much-needed help at the foot of Lovat Lane.

107. 'Up the hill'. Pulling and pushing towards Eastcheap.

Teabreak!

108. The aptly-named Piscatorial Café at the rear of the trading floor.

109. The convivial interior of the Café.

110. Porters enjoying a smoke and a mug of tea.

111. Sold out. The empty counter at 10.00 a.m.

Boiling & Freezing

112. Doomed crabs await their turn for the Boiling Shop.

113. The Boiling Shop, where all shellfish was instantly boiled in accordance with statutory requirements, before delivery to the purchaser.

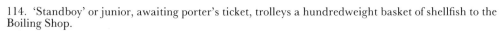

114. 'Standboy' or junior, awaiting porter's ticket, trolleys a hundredweight basket of shellfish to the Boiling Shop.

115. A brief pause for breath in the tropical heat of the shop.

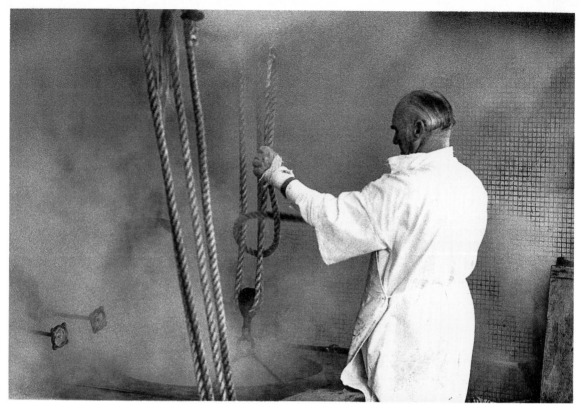

116. Clouds of scalding steam almost obscure the scene as shellfish are winched into a boiling cauldron.

117. Down in the basement: an extreme contrast in temperatures!

118. A heavily-clad porter manoeuvres fishboxes in the claustrophobic, sub-zero conditions of Billingsgate Coldstore.

119. Stacking fishboxes in the coldstore. This was built before modern insulation was developed and resembled a series of ice caves. The scene was probably unique and normally witnessed only by those who worked there.

120. Giant icicle. Any fish unsold at the end of the day was delivered to the coldstore for future sale at a slightly lower price.

121. The antiquated ammonia refrigeration plant. A badly-insulated pipe is thickly covered with ice.

122. Ice encrusts a refrigeration pipe installed immediately underneath the original groined and vaulted basement roof. The mezzanine floor was a later addition.

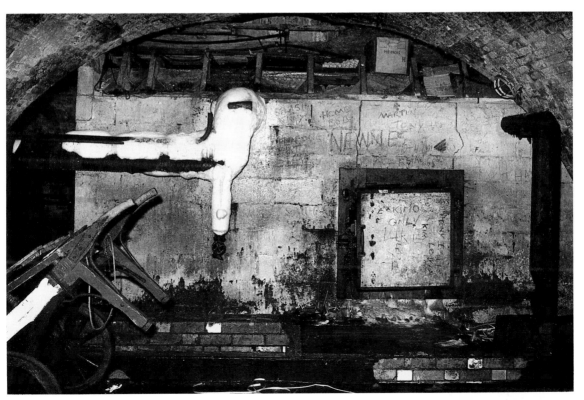

123. Liftmen worked the inadequate old lifts to the basement.

124. A porter wheels a barrow of fish from the basement lift exit.

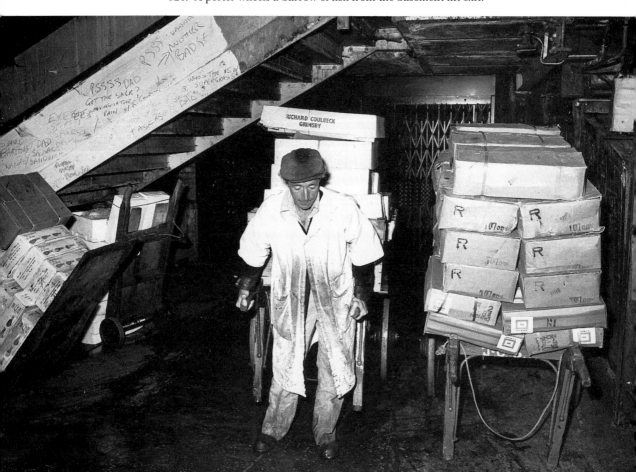

125. Some merchants rented modular coldrooms on the mezzanine floor.

126. A fish merchant checks the contents of a coldroom.

127. 'Tiger', the half wild Billingsgate cat, preferred the basement.

Skills & Secrets

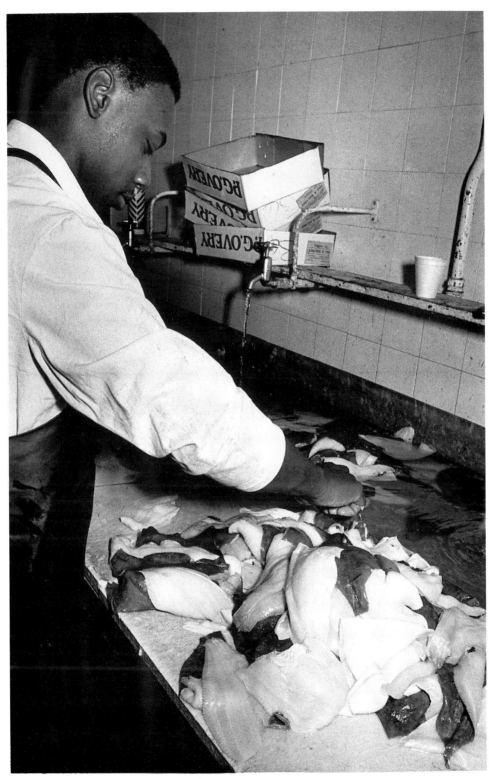

128. Fish filleting.

129. The Cutting Shop, where fish was filleted.

130. Fish filleting.

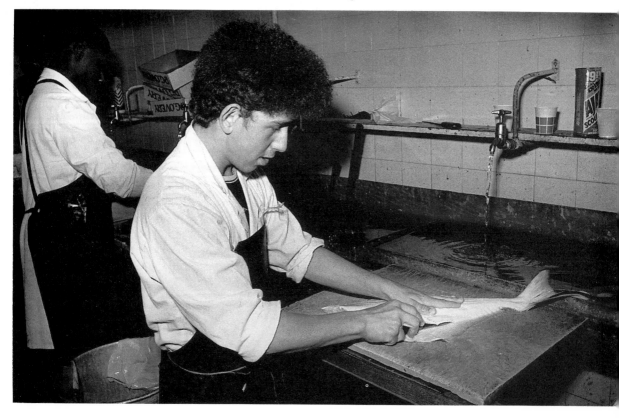

131. Mr. Seagrave of Brice Bros. explains the mysteries of storing live lobsters. This firm, founded in 1850, pioneered live lobster storage in London.

132. The safely locked premises of Brice Bros. at 13 The Quay, Billingsgate Market, where the lobster tanks were installed. (Out building since demolished.)

133. A privileged view of a lobster tank. The constituents of the artificial seawater which kept these monsters alive were a closely-guarded secret.

Local Firms : Fixing & Mending

134. Old fish merchants' premises, 16-20 Monument House, Monument Street. The ornate buildings, traditional wooden barrows and granite sets seemed to belong to the distant past, rather than to 1981, the year the photograph was taken.

135. Sidwell & McGrath Ltd. 'Ten yards from the Monument with our own, large cold store. No waiting'. In the 1950s there were 50 firms of fish merchants close to the market. By 1981, nearly all had closed.

136. A lorry load of fish delivered to Sidwell & McGrath.

137. V.J. Travis & Co. on the corner of Monument Street and Fish Street Hill.

138. C.T. Holmes, 40 Fish Street Hill. This entire block was demolished and replaced with offices, the present Nomura House and Gartmore House.

139. J. Williams & Son's truck in the lorry park. This long established family firm, based in Finsbury Park, was a frequent visitor to the market, repairing and maintaining merchants' barrows and trolleys.

140. A row of trolleys awaiting attention, each marked with the name of a fish merchant.

141. Painting a firm's name on a trolley. Low friction nylon wheels were fitted in readiness for the move to the new market.

142. Details of construction of a traditional market barrow, inscribed 'J. Williams, 2A Fonthill Road, N.4'. The firm subsequently moved to Surrey.

143. Baskets of overalls outside Billingsgate Overall Service, 13b Lovat Lane. Overalls took heavy punishment and were cleaned weekly by the small family firm. The building survives but has been renovated and converted to offices.

144. Aprons and overalls under repair in the basement workshop. An eyelet machine is in use on the right. Overalls were made from 10-12oz. cotton duck to a 30-year-old pattern and lasted between one and two years.

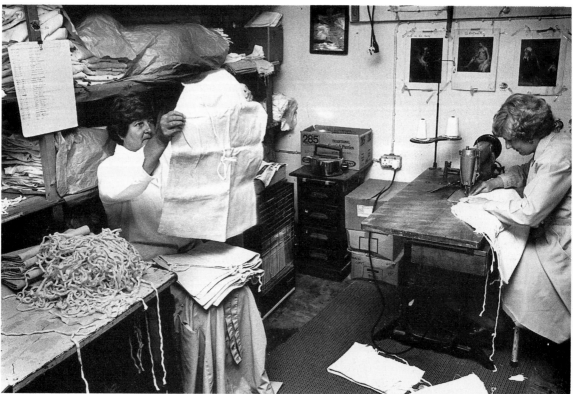

145. The storeroom. Overalls were sent out for cleaning on Tuesdays, received back on Wednesdays, sorted, stored and returned to the market on Fridays. Overalls were not owned by porters but hired by employers.

146. Mr. Branch, the proprietor, wheels clean overalls to the market, down Lovat Lane. This used to be called Love Lane.

147 Old sign at Billingsgate Christian Mission and Dispensary, 19 St Mary-at-Hill, which was founded *c*.1880. The Mission's original aim was to undertake Christian work and help the needy.

148. Billingsgate Christian Mission building on the corner of Monument Street and St Mary-at-Hill. The Mission developed an important role, providing medical treatment for the local workforce, which was once as high as 50,000, including market, wharves and warehouses.

149. Sister Davey comforting a vagrant in the Mission's treatment room.

150. A salesman receives first aid. Minor accidents were not infrequent at the market, although far fewer than the 20,000 cases per annum which the Mission once handled. The Mission was strongly supported by market people and still occupies the same building.

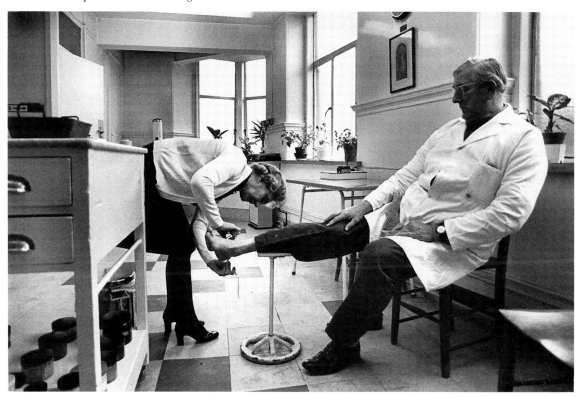

History & Tradition

151. Billingsgate Market bell, above the main entrance. The bell was still rung daily at 6.00 a.m. and 3.00 p.m. to indicate the official start and finish of business.

152. The vacated, padlocked and shuttered premises of R.W. Earkins & Co. Ltd., fish merchants, St Mary-at-Hill. This important building, once the ceremonial hall of the Fellowship Porters Company, was subsequently restored and preserved.

153. A collection of Billingsgate tokens preserved at the market offices. Tokens were paid in lieu of cash deposits on the returnable boxes in use until 1932. Some had rounded projections to prevent them from adhering when they became wet with fish slime.

Open Day

BILLINGSGATE MARKET
IS A
WHOLESALE MARKET
RETAIL SALES ARE
AVAILABLE AT NEARBY
LEADENHALL MARKET

C.A. WIARD.
SUPERINTENDENT.

154. As this old sign indicated, the public were not normally admitted to Billingsgate.

155. Visitors were welcomed on annual open days. These crowds were queueing for 'The Wonderful World of Fish' Exhibition, September 1980.

156. An important visitor, the Lord Mayor of London, Sir Peter Gadsden, samples an oyster, encouraged by Mr. Butcher, the Market Superintendent.

157. A Billingsgate porter, immaculately turned out for the occasion, resplendent in bobbin hat, enamel licence badge and spotless smock.

158. Fish filleting competition. Finalists had 20 minutes to skin and curl a whiting; wing and skin a whole skate; fillet a witch/megrim; steak a cod; skin and trim a lemon sole and bone a herring.

159. A salesman explains one of the elaborate fish displays.

160. A fish display arranged by Portch's, the well-known West London fishmongers.

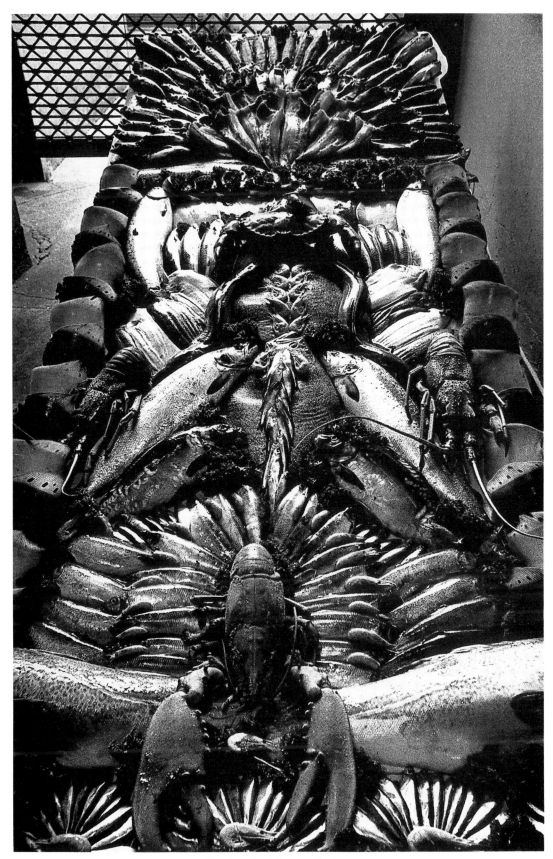

161. A truly elaborate display.

162. 'Give me a kiss and I'm Jaws.'

163. A fishmonger's macabre sense of humour. Shark and the filleted specimens were auctioned for charity.

164. Salesman's pun, 'I'm hooked on fish'.

Closure

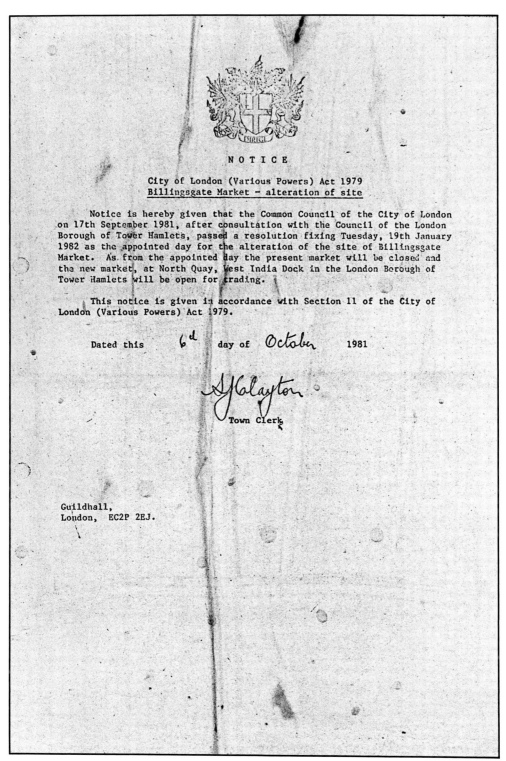

N O T I C E

City of London (Various Powers) Act 1979
Billingsgate Market – alteration of site

Notice is hereby given that the Common Council of the City of London on 17th September 1981, after consultation with the Council of the London Borough of Tower Hamlets, passed a resolution fixing Tuesday, 19th January 1982 as the appointed day for the alteration of the site of Billingsgate Market. As from the appointed day the present market will be closed and the new market, at North Quay, West India Dock in the London Borough of Tower Hamlets will be open for trading.

This notice is given in accordance with Section 11 of the City of London (Various Powers) Act 1979.

Dated this   6ᵈ   day of   October   1981

A J Clayton
Town Clerk

Guildhall,
London, EC2P 2EJ.

165. Official notice of Billingsgate's closure and transfer from the City to the new site in Tower Hamlets, 19 January 1982.

166. Closing time. Piscatorial Café.

167. Shutters down. The empty trading floor reflects the silhouettes of the arcades.